B is for Badger

A Wisconsin Alphabet

Written by Kathy-jo Wargin and Illustrated by Renée Graef

Sleeping Bear Press™

2395 South Huron Parkway, Suite 200
Ann Arbor, MI 48104
www.sleepingbearpress.com

Printed and bound in the United States.

16 15 14

Library of Congress Cataloging-in-Publication Data

Wargin, Kathy-Jo.
B is for Badger : a Wisconsin alphabet / written by Kathy-Jo Wargin;
illustrated by Renée Graef.
p. cm.
ISBN 978-1-58536-135-9
1. Wisconsin—Juvenile literature. 2. English
language—Alphabet—Juvenile literature. [1. Wisconsin. 2. Alphabet.]
I. Graef, Renée, ill. II. Title.
F581.3 .W37 2004
428.1—dc22
[E]
2003026230

To all Warden and Nelson relatives in Wisconsin, descendents of my great-grandfather Frank Warden from Monroe, Wisconsin.

KATHY-JO

To Wisconsin Public Radio, a true Wisconsin and national treasure.

RENÉE

The American Water Spaniel was adopted as the official state dog of Wisconsin in 1985. As the only dog native to Wisconsin, it is believed to be one of only five dogs native to the United States. The breed came to be when waterfowl hunters developed a hunting dog with a warm, thick coat that could fit easily into a small boat and stay warm during hunting adventures. Not only is the American Water Spaniel a good hunting dog, its small size and easygoing temperament make it a wonderful family pet as well.

A is also for the Apostle Islands National Lakeshore, a group of 21 islands that form a federal preserve area on the northwestern Bayfield Peninsula. Rich in history and natural beauty, the islands are a wonderful place to visit, but can only be reached by boat.

A is American Water Spaniel
riding in a boat.
This native of Wisconsin
has a warm and curly coat.

The badger was adopted as the official state animal of Wisconsin in 1957. Wisconsin earned the nickname "The Badger State" in the early 1800s when miners were so busy mining for lead that they used abandoned mine shafts for homes, or carved dens into the hillsides, much like the burrowing animal, the badger. Over time, the term "badger" became a nickname for the people of Wisconsin, and eventually people began to call Wisconsin "The Badger State."

B is for Badger—
   Our nickname was found
when hardworking miners
      made homes in the ground.

Cc

The North American cranberry, or *Vaccinium macrocarpon*, is a low-growing woody perennial plant with small ovate leaves, and is Wisconsin's top fruit crop. Producing more than 300 million pounds of cranberries each year, Wisconsin is the leading producer of cranberries in the United States. Harvest typically takes place in September and October. A wet harvest is when the beds where cranberries grow are flooded and cranberries float to the surface where they can be scooped up. A dry harvest is when the fruit is pulled from its vines using a special machine. In 1860 Edward Sacket began cultivating cranberries near Berlin, Wisconsin. Today there are more than 200 cranberry marshes in 18 Wisconsin counties.

CRANBERRIES

C is for Cranberries
floating on top.
We harvest the most
of this lovely red crop.

And **D** is for Dairy cow
grazing afar.
"America's Dairyland"
is what we are.

Moo! Moo! I like milk, do you?

The dairy cow is Wisconsin's state domesticated animal. Wisconsin has long been referred to as "America's Dairyland" because it produces more milk than any other state. In addition it is the leading producer of cheese in the nation and was the first state to produce two popular cheeses: Colby and Brick. It's not surprising that milk is Wisconsin's state beverage!

D is also for beautiful Door County with its state parks, lighthouses, and miles and miles of shoreline.

Wisconsin has many effigy sites. An effigy is a mound made by Native Americans long ago, most often in the shape of animals or other geometric emblems. They were created using soil, and most of them date back more than one thousand years. Many of them served as ancient burial sites for the Mississippian and Woodland cultures that lived in Wisconsin long ago.

BIRD

E e

E is for the Effigy—
It's a pretty mound
that's shaped just like an animal
and made upon the ground.

F f

And **F** is for a famous man,
his name is Frank Lloyd Wright.
Designer of a "Prairie Style,"
his buildings look just right!

Frank Lloyd Wright was born in Richland Center in 1867, and is known as one of the world's most influential architects of all time. His belief "form and function are one" inspired many noted buildings, including his Spring Green home called Taliesin, the Larkin Company Administration Building in Buffalo, New York, and the Guggenheim Museum in New York City. Frank Lloyd Wright died at age 92 in the year 1959. He designed approximately 1,000 structures, nearly 400 of which were built.

FALLING WA

GUGGENHEIM

Gg

Galena starts with letter **G**.
This mineral we all know
    attracted settlers to our state
so many years ago.

And Georgia O'Keeffe begins with **G**.
This artist we all know
    was born in our Wisconsin
more than one hundred years ago.

GALENA=

LEAD

Wisconsin's state mineral is galena, otherwise known as lead. The proposal to adopt galena as the state mineral was initiated by the Kenosha Gem and Mineral Society, because galena was the mineral to first attract miners and settlers to Wisconsin.

Georgia O'Keeffe was born on November 15, 1887, on a farm in Sun Prairie, Wisconsin. She loved and practiced art as a young child, and went on to study at the Art Institute of Chicago from 1905 to 1906, and then went to the Art Students League in New York from 1907 to 1908. From that time on she spent her time either studying or teaching at many different schools, until the spring of 1918 when photographer Alfred Stieglitz offered her a chance to paint in New York for one year. In 1924 Stieglitz and O'Keeffe were married, living and working together in New York. Some of Georgia O'Keeffe's most noted and recognized pictures are large-scale depictions of flowers, and scenes from New Mexico. She died in 1986 at the age of 98.

And **H** is for the Horicon Marsh,
the largest one of all.
A wetland filled with cattails
attracts birds big and small.

Horicon Marsh is approximately 32,000 acres in size, making it one of the largest freshwater marshes in the United States. Filled with cattails as well as open water, it is a haven for wildlife and birds such as rough-legged hawks, northern harriers, horned larks, great blue herons, Canada geese, bald eagles, and yellow warblers. In 1991 the marsh was dedicated as only one of 15 wetlands in the U.S. to be noted as a "wetland of international importance."

Nearly every prehistoric Indian culture of the upper Midwest in the last 10 to 12 thousand years has either used or lived near Horicon Marsh. We know this by artifacts left behind such as Indian spear points, stone tools, arrowheads, and effigy mounds. When white men first settled in the area, they referred to the area as "The Great Marsh of the Winnebagos."

H h

The Ice Age National Scenic Trail is a wonderful way to experience varied landforms left by glaciers more than 10,000 years ago. As the last glacier melted and retreated, it split into six major lobes (rounded divisions) that spread across the state creating lakes, moraines, ridges, and hills as well as bogs, marshes, and streams. The Ice Age Trail is a thousand-mile national and state scenic trail located entirely in Wisconsin.

I i

The letter I is Ice Age Trail
where you can walk through time.
Come learn about the glaciers
and the land they left behind.

John Muir (1838-1914) was a famous explorer, writer, and naturalist. Although born in Scotland, he spent his boyhood days on a family farm in Fountain Lake, and then studied at the University of Wisconsin. He became the first president and founder of the Sierra Club, an organization dedicated to preserving important natural areas in our country. Known to many as the "father" of the conservation movement and also of our national park system, Muir was instrumental in the creation of many national parks including Yosemite and Sequoia. Today the area where he grew up is primarily preserved as the John Muir Memorial Park.

Another famous figure in conservation is Aldo Leopold (1887-1948). Born near Burlington, Iowa, he came to Madison in 1924 to work for the U.S. Forest Products Laboratory, and by 1928 was teaching at the University of Wisconsin. Leopold is often acknowledged as the "father" of wildlife ecology due in part to his 1933 book *Game Management*, which outlined the skills necessary for managing and restoring wildlife. His *A Sand County Almanac* is known by millions throughout the world, and has led many people to learn about living in harmony and balance with the land.

John Muir starts with letter J—
The "father of conservation"
created many parks that are
important to our nation.

k

K

The letter **K** is Kindergarten,
that's what people say.
Did you know it started here?
We love it yet today!

Margarethe Meyer Schurz started the first kindergarten in the United States in Watertown in 1856. Margarethe, born in Germany, taught school in the United Kingdom, and when she and her husband Carl Schurz moved to Wisconsin, she began to teach her daughter and other young children. This effort was the beginning of kindergarten as we know it today. The building where kindergarten began is now an historic site maintained by the Watertown Historic Society.

A-B-C and 1-2-3!
Can you skip along with me?

Wisconsin is flanked by two of the five Great Lakes, Lake Michigan and Lake Superior. With an average depth of 500 feet, Lake Superior, or "Gitchee Gummee" as it is called in myth and legend, is not only the largest and coldest of the Great Lakes, but also has the largest freshwater surface area in the world. Lake Michigan ranks third out of the five Great Lakes by surface area, and is the sixth largest freshwater lake in the world.

L l

L is for Lake Michigan
        and Lake Superior, too.
They are big and beautiful
        and we all love the view! So blue!

M m

Now Madison begins with **M**,
a capital for our state.
Here the rules and laws are made
that make Wisconsin great!

Our capital city Madison is named for the fourth president of the United States, James Madison. In 1836, after President Andrew Jackson created the Territory of Wisconsin, the first governor of the Territory, Henry Dodge, convened the first legislature to discuss where the capital should be. In that same year, a bill was passed to locate the seat of government in Madison.

In 1955 the Muskellunge, or *Esox masquinongy Mitchell*, was named the official state fish of Wisconsin. A member of the pike family, the "Muskie" is a large fish with very sharp canine teeth on the lower jaw. If you visit the National Fresh Water Fishing Hall of Fame & Museum in Hayward, you can walk through a very big Muskie!

m
M

And **M** is also for a fish,
the Muskie is its name.
Come and learn about it
in the Fishing Hall of Fame!

Swish! Swish! Oh, what a fish!

N is for the Native culture,
　　　　roots from long ago.
And also for the Northwoods,
　　　　it's where the pine trees grow.

Deer, moose, and bear—
Over here, over there!

Wisconsin's current Native American population has the greatest variety of distinct Indian societies east of the Mississippi River. The culture of Native Americans from Ottawa, Ojibwa, Winnebago, Potawatomi, Sauk, and others have made significant contributions to the names and places we know today. The Native American word for Wisconsin means a "gathering of waters" and was later translated by the French into "Ouisconsin."

The spirit of the "northwoods" has long been adopted into the spirit of Wisconsin. The abundance of northern forests make ideal habitats for many woodland creatures such as deer, bear, moose, and wolves, making it a wonderful place to explore nature. And with about 90% of Wisconsin's lakes, the northern region is a popular vacation destination.

N n

The Wisconsin state song was adopted in 1959 and is titled "On, Wisconsin." Initially written in 1909 by William T. Purdy, the words were changed in 1913 by J.S. Hubbard and Charles D. Rosa to acknowledge the centennial of the Battle of Lake Erie. In 1959 when the song was officially recognized as the state song it was discovered that there were many different versions of lyrics, so an official text for the first verse was used.

"On, Wisconsin! On, Wisconsin!
Grand old badger state!
We, thy loyal sons and daughters,
Hail thee, good and great.
On, Wisconsin! On, Wisconsin!
Champion of the right,
'Forward,' our motto
God will give thee might!"

O is for "On, Wisconsin."
It's a song we love to sing.
It's the anthem for our state,
let our voices ring!

P p

Now **P** is for our favorite team.
Shout **P** is for the Packers!
And **P** is for the greatest fans.
They're called the Packer-Backers!
Go, Green Bay, Go!

In 1919 Earl Louis Lambeau and George Calhoun organized a football team named the Packers with support from the Indian Packing Company, which provided money for jerseys and the use of its field. Eventually, the meatpacking company ceased to support the team, and shares for the Packers were sold to Green Bay businesses. Today the Packers are the only publicly owned team in the National Football League, and that is evident in the loyal and extreme support given by the fans.

Q is Quadracci Pavilion,
    the building is one of a kind.
At the Milwaukee Art Museum,
    come see what you can find.

The Quadracci Pavilion was designed by Santiago Calatrava, and is a unique structure which combines art, dramatic architecture, and landscape design. As part of the Milwaukee Art Museum's expansion, the Quadracci Pavilion was unveiled in May of 2001. The first building in the United States to be designed by Calatrava, its special features include a 90-foot-high glass-walled reception hall and a suspended pedestrian bridge with a 200-foot-tall angled mast and cables, making it a creative environment to view great collections of art and artistry.

Q q

And **R** is for the Robin sweet,
it tells us spring is here.
And also for the Ringling Brothers,
stars of circus cheer!

R r

The American robin is Wisconsin's official state bird. In 1926-27, school-children voted for the robin as Wisconsin's state bird, but it wasn't until 1949 when it actually became the official state bird of Wisconsin. The robin was chosen because it represents the birth of spring and the awakening of nature after a long, cold, and hard winter.

The Ringling Bros. Circus was founded in Baraboo, Wisconsin, in 1884 by five brothers: Al, Otto, Charles, John, and Alf T. Ringling. In 1907 they purchased their competitor, the Barnum & Bailey Show, and in 1918 merged the two shows into one new circus, known as "The Greatest Show on Earth."

The letter **S** is Summerfest Grounds.
Wisconsin comes together
to share our music, food, and more
in any kind of weather.

S is also Sugar maple—
And we think it's neat
a tree can give us maple syrup,
rich and thick and sweet.
Yum! Yum!

The Summerfest Grounds, also known as Maier Festival Park, is a gathering place for people to celebrate music, art, and culture. A 90-acre park along Lake Michigan, it began as a vision of the late Mayor Henry W. Maier in the 1960s as a place for people to meet and a way to energize downtown Milwaukee. Summerfest Grounds is also home to Summerfest, the largest music festival in the world.

Wisconsin's official state tree since 1949, the sugar maple, *Acer saccharum*, is also known as the hard or rock maple, and is one of more than 200 species in the maple family. An important hardwood, it is found throughout much of northeastern and midwestern America. The sugar maple has deeply indented leaves, can reach heights of 130 feet or more, and will often live to be very old. It is also known for the syrup and sugar made from its sap, which has higher concentrations of sugar than other maple trees. This results in lighter, better-tasting syrup.

Ss

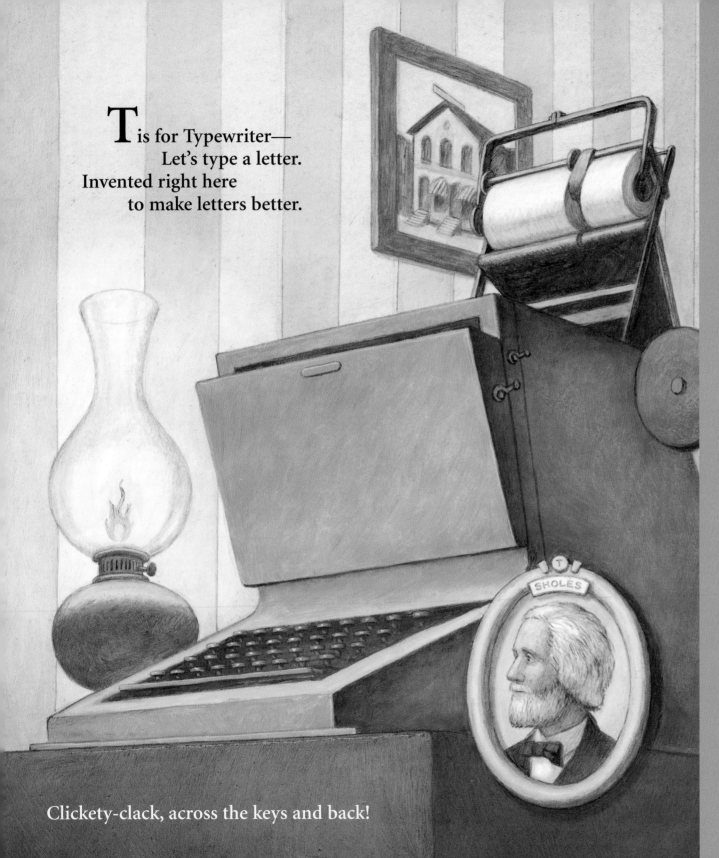

T is for Typewriter—
Let's type a letter.
Invented right here
to make letters better.

Clickety-clack, across the keys and back!

Christopher Latham Sholes, Carlos Glidden, and S.W. Soule of Milwaukee patented the first typewriter in 1867. Eventually this model served as the prototype for the first commercially produced typewriter called the Sholes and Glidden model. Available for sale in 1874, it wrote in capitals only. In 1878 a shift key was introduced to type lowercase letters as well. The layout of the keys, called the QWERTY keyboard, is the same pattern used on all keyboards today.

The University of Wisconsin
starts with letter U.
The first radio station in our nation
made sounds from here—It's true!

In 1915 an experimental station at the University of Wisconsin began transmitting radio signals, and a marker at the university calls it the "oldest station in the nation."

In 1914 Professor Edward Bennet set up a wireless telegraphic system and secured a license for what was then called 9XM. Joined by physics professor Earle M. Terry, the experimental station evolved and in December of 1916, sent out a dot-and-dash version of a weather forecast. In 1917 they experimented with the broadcast of musical recordings, and regularly scheduled voice broadcasts began in February of 1920. In 1922, when the station was relicensed, the call letters were changed to WHA.

BASCOM HALL

WHA

U
u

Now V is for the Violet,
delicate and sweet,
growing in the forest
right beneath our feet.

The wood violet is Wisconsin's official state flower. In 1908 schoolchildren voting for a state flower selected four finalists: the wood violet, wild rose, trailing arbutus, and the white water lily. The wood violet won the final vote in 1909, but it remained unofficial until 1948 when it was adopted as the official state flower of Wisconsin. The wood violet, or *Viola papilionacea*, can be found throughout the woods, meadows, and roadsides of Wisconsin. This lovely flower blooms in spring and early summer.

And **W** is for White-tailed deer,
it makes its home right here.
And also for Wisconsin Dells
where rocks and cliffs are near.

The Wisconsin Dells are a beautiful portion of the Wisconsin River, where the river has cut a deep gorge into the sandstone, creating caves and shapes. Long ago, the region appeared on maps as the "Dalles" but was later Anglicized as the "dells." Today the Wisconsin Dells are a vacation destination, boasting theme parks, natural attractions, and boat rides.

The white-tailed deer is an abundant Wisconsin mammal, and was named the official state wildlife animal in 1957. As the most abundant big game animal in North America, the white-tailed deer, or *odocoileus virginianus*, is a familiar sight for most Wisconsinites.

STAND ROCK

WITCHES GULCH

W
W

The American Birkebeiner, a famous cross-country ski race, is held every winter between Hayward and Cable, Wisconsin. In 1206 in Norway, during the Norwegian Civil War, Birkebeiner skiers made their way through the forests and mountains of the Osterdalen valley, carrying the son of King Sverresson and Inga of Vartieg from Lillehammer to safety in the town of Trondheim. Eventually, the little boy became King Hakon Hakonsson IV, and was a great influence on northern European history.

The first race to commemorate this event from Norwegian history took place in Norway in 1932, and the word Birkebeiner means "birch-bark leggings." Today, races commemorating the event take place in Norway, Canada, and the United States.

X is for X-country ski.
We hold the largest race.
It's called the Birkebeiner.
Look who's in first place.

Oh my, you're passing me by!

Yy

Yellow fields of corn dominate the Wisconsin landscape, where corn is the official state grain. It was adopted in 1989 to make people aware of its importance as a cash crop in Wisconsin's economy.

The official design for the state flag was adopted in 1863, but was changed in 1913, giving the flag a dark blue background with a state coat of arms centered at each side. In 1979 the design was changed again, and the word Wisconsin and the date 1848 were added. The coat of arms in the center shows the state motto "Forward," and the yellow shield in the center shows Wisconsin's support for the United States. There are four sections that surround the shield and they represent Wisconsin's main industries: agriculture, mining, manufacturing, and navigation. There is also a sailor and a miner to represent how people of Wisconsin work on water and land.

Y is for the Yellow corn
sitting on my plate.
Wisconsin grows the most of this
and we think it tastes great!

And Y is for the Yellow shield,
our flag could not be finer.
It's in the very middle
with the sailor and the miner.

The letter Z is for the Zoo.
      With many in our state
   we can visit every one
         and we think it's really great!

And there you have the ABCs.
It seems our work is done.
We've learned about Wisconsin
and we've all had lots of fun!

Wisconsin has a rich heritage of creating and maintaining wonderful zoos, and they are all great places to explore interesting animals and their habitats. The Henry Vilas Zoo in Madison created its first animal exhibits in 1911, and the Milwaukee County Zoo, which is home to approximately 2,500 animals, began as a mammal and bird display in 1892. That's more than 100 years of zoo history! There are also many other zoos in Wisconsin, and it is fun to try to visit them all.

Zz

Questions & Answers for Little Badgers

1. This freshwater marsh is approximately 32,000 acres in size, making it one of the largest in the U.S. What is its name?

2. Which of the Great Lakes has the nickname of "Gitchee Gummee"?

3. Name the professional football team that was originally supported by the Indian Packing Company?

4. What famous cross-country ski race is held every winter between Hayward and Cable, Wisconsin?

5. Our state dog loves the water, has a thick warm coat, and is the only dog native to Wisconsin. What is its name?

6. What is Wisconsin's top fruit crop? Hint: It is a low-growing plant with bright red berries.

7. Our state fish is not pretty, with its sharp canine teeth on its lower jaw. What is it?

8. What is the name of our state capital city? Hint: It is named for a former president of the United States.

9. This machine was first patented in Wisconsin and has certainly helped making letter writing a lot easier. What is this machine?

10. Hardworking miners helped contribute to our state nickname. What is it?

11. The dairy cow, our state domesticated animal, is a good representative of Wisconsin. Why?

12. These animal-shaped mounds of earth were made long ago by Native Americans. What are these mounds called?

13. What state symbol represents the birth of spring and the awakening of nature after a long, cold winter?

14. Who was the Wisconsin resident who founded the Sierra Club and is viewed by many as the "father" of the nature movement?

1. Horicon Marsh

2. Lake Superior has the nickname of "Gitchee Gummee" and is the largest and coldest of the Great Lakes.

3. The Green Bay Packers

4. The American Birkebeiner

5. The American Water Spaniel

6. The North American cranberry is Wisconsin's top fruit crop.

7. The Muskellunge or "muskie" as it's commonly called.

8. Our capital city is Madison.

9. The typewriter

10. Wisconsin is called "The Badger State."

11. Wisconsin produces more milk than any other state, as well as being the leading producer of cheese.

12. These mounds are called effigies.

13. The robin, our state bird.

14. John Muir

Kathy-jo Wargin

Author Kathy-jo Wargin has earned national acclaim with numerous best-selling children's titles, including *The Edmund Fitzgerald: Song of the Bell*. Born in Tower, Minnesota, Kathy-jo has spent a great deal of time in the upper Midwest. Previously, she teamed up with illustrator Gijsbert van Frankenhuyzen on the award-winning *Legends* series, including *The Legend of Sleeping Bear* and *The Legend of the Lady's Slipper* (Upper Midwest Bookseller's Favorite). *B is for Badger* is her fourth state alphabet book. She is a frequent lecturer and guest speaker throughout the country. Kathy-jo lives with her family in Petoskey, Michigan. You can learn more about her at www.edwargin.com.

Renée Graef

Renée Graef is new to the Sleeping Bear Press family but is very well known as the children's book illustrator for the "Kirsten" books in the *American Girl* collection. She has also illustrated many books in the *My First Little House* series with HarperCollins. Renée received her bachelor's degree in art from the University of Wisconsin-Madison. She lives in Cedarburg, Wisconsin, with her family.